Original title:
The Caregiver's Song

Copyright © 2025 Creative Arts Management OÜ
All rights reserved.

Author: Vivian Laurent
ISBN HARDBACK: 978-1-80581-878-6
ISBN PAPERBACK: 978-1-80581-405-4
ISBN EBOOK: 978-1-80581-878-6

The Beat of Understanding

In the kitchen chaos, I dance, tap my feet,
With a pot as a drum, my rhythm's a treat.
A sprinkle of laughter, a dash of delight,
Cooking up joy in the soft morning light.

Oh, socks in the dryer, a mystery spree,
Where do they vanish? It's just socks, you see!
Chasing elusive fabric, a funny old game,
Yet somehow together, we're all still the same.

When spills happen, oh, what a delight,
I slip and I slide, what a comedic sight!
A laugh and a shrug, not a moment to waste,
With each little blunder, it's joy we embrace.

At bedtime, we giggle, the day's work is done,
Tales of the wild, of laughter and fun.
As dreams flutter in, with a wink and a grin,
Tomorrow awaits, more adventures begin!

Echoes of Nurturing Hands

In the kitchen, pots go clang,
Spaghetti ninja leaps with a twang.
A recipe calls, but I just toss,
Silly little mess, oh what a loss.

Banana peels slip like a dance,
Every floor's a chance for a prance.
Cooking chaos, laughter fills the air,
A spattering chef, heart laid bare.

Harmonies of Healing

With a splash of humor, I swipe the dust,
Cleaning chores, but laughter's a must.
Singing to plants, they sway with glee,
'The more, the merrier!' they chant with me.

My cat rolls over, takes up the stage,
Paws on the keyboard, what a funny mage.
Naps in the sun are a serious sport,
As I tut and giggle, the day's my court.

The Symphony of Support

In socks mismatched, I trounce around,
Finding lost treasures, what joy I've found.
Armchair debates with my playful pup,
As he nods wisely, I can't give up.

Juggling laundry like it's a show,
I toss a shirt, where will it go?
A sock escapes, jumps off the shelf,
'Is that a bird?' I laugh at myself.

Serenade of Sentiment

In the garden, weeds wear hats,
While I sing tunes to the friendly rats.
Sunflowers listen, nodding to the beats,
I dance like nobody's around, what a feat!

Rainy days bring puddles grand,
Splashing in boots, it's all unplanned.
Every droplet's a giggle, sweet and light,
As I stomp through the squishy delight.

Breathe in Love

In the chaos, I find my shoes,
Each morning feels like a ruse.
Coffee spills on my favorite dress,
Yet I smile, what a funny mess!

Sock monsters sneak all day long,
My laundry basket sings a song.
Laughter echoes down these halls,
Where love's the cure for pesky falls.

Chasing giggles, I trip and spin,
Finding joy in the silliest grin.
With every hug, my heart will dance,
Life is better with a child's glance.

Notes Woven from Affection

I promise not to burn the bread,
But somehow it's a daily spread.
Pasta sticks, oh, what a sight,
Gourmet chef? More like a fright!

I sing a song to make them cheer,
Sounding like a squeaky deer.
But in this house, we have a band,
Making music, not so bland!

Invisible ink on their foreheads,
I write reminders of my threads.
Forget the salad, oh what a blunder,
We'll laugh at our delicious wonder!

A Canvas of Care

With crayons, they create their art,
Masterpieces that steal my heart.
Walls are covered, floor's a mess,
Oops! There goes my favorite dress!

I wield a brush, paint in hand,
Create with chaos, oh isn't it grand?
Splashes of red and swirls of blue,
Looks like a wild party for two!

Every painting tells a tale,
Of coffee spills and epic fails.
Yet love's the color that shines bright,
In this crazy, joyful light.

Nurturing Echoes

When bedtime calls, it's quite the race,
To find the shoes, the books, the space.
Stories tangled in giggles deep,
While monsters plot and shadows creep.

With every 'just one more' plea,
I feel the night devour me.
But laughter lights up the gloomy dark,
As we play whispers in the park.

Their dreams take flight, oh what a joy,
Every giggle from my little boy.
And in their world, I see it clear,
Love blooms brightly, year by year.

Harmonies of Healing

With a spatula in hand, I sing,
Mixing potions as the children cling.
"Eat your veggies!" I boldly chime,
While dodging toys—it's a slippery climb.

Songs of giggles fill the air,
As I trip over teddy bears with flair.
"Who needs sleep? I'm wide awake!"
Juggling chaos like a piece of cake.

Whispers in the Night

Moonlight sneaks in with a grin,
While I sneak snacks, oh what a sin!
Whispers of lullabies, soft and low,
But wait! Is that a sock? Oh no, oh no!

A shadow creeps past, a munchy fright,
Snack attacks, my midnight delight.
I hum a tune, it's calm and sweet,
While monsters under beds run for a treat.

The Heart's Embrace

Hugs are my superpower, it's true,
With each cuddle, I'm free to renew.
Crafty chaos, with crayons and glue,
What's that? A masterpiece? Shh, it's blue!

Silly dances break the dull mood,
Guess what? Birthday cake every dude!
With each tickle fight, and snorty laugh,
I'm the captain of this goofy craft!

Lullabies of Love

Singing softly at day's sweet close,
As bath time turns to splashy prose.
Rubber ducks quack in a rhythmic spree,
With bubble beards, they dance merrily.

In this symphony of playful care,
I talk to walls like they'd really share.
But who needs sleep? Not me, not now!
Let's sing 'til morning, oh, take a bow!

Bridges Built on Kindness

In a world of spilled milk, I sweep and I sigh,
I juggle my worries, give it a try.
With a broom and a wink, I conquer my day,
Building bridges of kindness, come laugh, come play.

I wear mismatched socks, it's my fashion spree,
Who needs the catwalk when you have me?
With each quirk and giggle, we share a light,
Creating our laughter, both day and night.

Illuminating Hearts

With a microwave dance and a spatula spin,
I sauté my worries, let the fun begin.
In a kitchen of chaos, we whip up some cheer,
Turning burnt toast to laughter, the recipe's clear.

With a band of band-aids and a glue stick or two,
We craft a fine mess of glittery goo.
It's a party of mishaps, let's toast to the fun,
With love that's contagious, we shine like the sun.

Fleeting Moments of Mending

In the tapestry of life, we patch with a grin,
A needle of humor, let the stitches begin.
With mismatched threads, we mend every seam,
Dancing through moments, united we dream.

In fleeting moments, we share and we play,
Turning mishaps to magic, come join our ballet.
With a tickle, a tease, we banish the gloom,
In this circus of caring, all are welcome to bloom.

Starlight and Solace

Underneath the stars, we gather and chat,
With laughter like fireflies, imagine that!
We make constellations from last night's pizza,
In the glow of our joy, even worries dissolve.

With a wink at the moon, we dance on the grass,
Creating a spectacle as shadows amass.
In our whimsical world of giggles and jokes,
Starlight and solace, our bond's no hoax.

Cradled by Kindness

In fluffy socks and mismatched shoes,
A dance of joy, they cannot lose.
With silly hats and playful grins,
They share a laugh, where joy begins.

A spoon to serve some chocolate cake,
A giggle shared for humor's sake.
With hugs so tight, the troubles flee,
They turn a frown to jubilee.

A wink, a nudge, a playful jest,
They spread delight, and feel the zest.
When life gets tough, they take it light,
And turn the day from dull to bright.

In every moment, laughter's found,
A happy heart is quite profound.
With kindness wrapped in laughter strong,
They make the world a brighter song.

A Bouquet of Healing Words

With gentle phrases like a breeze,
They weave their magic, hearts at ease.
A pun, a joke, a joyful cheer,
Turns every frown into a deer.

With words that dance like flowers bloom,
They banish shadows, clear the gloom.
In laughter's bloom, the spirit sings,
A garden filled with wondrous things.

They sprinkle joy with every line,
A twist of humor, oh so fine.
A bouquet tied with bows of fun,
They light the way, a golden sun.

So gather 'round, let's share some cheer,
With healing words that draw us near.
In every chuckle, care is shared,
Together, love's bouquet is bared.

The Essence of Nurturing

With cookies baked and stories spun,
They turn the mundane into fun.
A sprinkle of joy in every task,
In silly faces, smiles unmask.

With apron on and spatula in hand,
They whip up joy that's simply grand.
In every hug, they nurture hearts,
And weave together clever arts.

A fortune cookie filled with jokes,
They lift the spirits of tired folks.
With laughter echoing all around,
In nurturing's warmth, love is found.

So dance a little, laugh a lot,
Life's too short to be forgot.
With kindness shared and humor bright,
They turn the dark into pure light.

Sails of Support

With paper boats and cheeky sails,
They navigate through wind and gales.
With witty quips as their own wind,
They guide the lost, with laughter pinned.

Through seas of troubles, they provide,
A buoyant laugh, a joyful ride.
With every wave, they lift and cheer,
In playful banter, love is near.

In storms of life, they stay afloat,
With silly antics, they promote.
Their sails of support, so well designed,
Keep spirits high and hearts aligned.

So hoist the flags, let laughter reign,
In every jest, there's joy to gain.
With sails of love and kindness strong,
They carry us across life's song.

A Dance with Diligence

In the kitchen, pots collide,
As I stir the soup with pride.
My dog thinks it's time for fun,
Chasing tails, oh what a run!

Laundry spinning like a dance,
Socks are lost, they take a chance.
Toys are scattered on the floor,
Oh look, another squeaky score!

Wipe the nose, then knock a cup,
With a laugh, I just don't stop.
Bubbles fly and laughter roars,
Who knew chores could be such scores?

At the end, we drop like flies,
Tired giggles, sleepy sighs.
In the chaos, love shines through,
This jolly life is quite the view!

Cadence of Compassion

Each morning's like a circus parade,
With breakfast chaos nicely laid.
Oatmeal here and toast that flies,
Sticky fingers, what a surprise!

Sneaky pets join in the fun,
As I chase them, I can't outrun.
Cuddles, giggles, and silly sounds,
Life's a dance in joyful bounds!

Homework battles, laughter ensues,
Crayons drawing wild blues and hues.
Smiles exchanged like secret codes,
Through the mess, love explodes!

At the day's end, hugs abound,
As stories weave, we're tightly bound.
In this symphony of care,
Together we dance, light as air!

Heartstrings of Hope

Tickle time, oh what a mess,
With giggles bursting, who could guess?
On the floor, we tumble and roll,
In this warmth, I find my soul.

Pillows stacked like towers tall,
A fort created, we'll never fall.
Adventure calls and off we go,
Through imagination's steady flow!

Tiny hands that reach for mine,
In this chaos, everything's fine.
We create laughter, loud and bright,
Each moment feels perfectly right.

As the moon begins to rise,
I see the joy in little eyes.
With heartstrings played in light staccato,
This funny life is a sweet bravado!

Chords of Care

Banana peels on the floor,
Oops! Slipped right out the door.
With a grin, I scrape the scene,
Life's a show, oh what a dream!

In the garden, mud pies made,
With sticky fingers, roles well played.
Jumping puddles, squeals of glee,
Such sweet chaos, wild and free!

Sippy cups and crayons roll,
Each little mishap takes its toll.
But laughter's the melody we hear,
In this concert, joy is clear.

As bedtime whispers sweetly near,
With stories told and a loving cheer.
In the symphony of night and day,
Love's the music, come what may!

Whispers of Tenderness

In the kitchen, pots do dance,
Cookies hide, they take a chance.
Broccoli wears a happy face,
While peas run off to hide, what a race!

In the garden, blooms all giggle,
Tangled vines start to wiggle.
With watering cans strutting about,
Even daisies have their doubts!

Chasing shadows, laughter flies,
Butterflies in fancy ties.
When the dog decides to bark,
Everyone joins in the lark!

At nap time, snoring loud,
Pillows wave to the snoring crowd.
With teddy bears holding a court,
What a sight in that sleep resort!

Melodies of Compassion

Under the stars, sneakers squeak,
Pirates search for treasure to seek.
While kids giggle and play their plight,
A cat rehearses for Broadway tonight!

In the park, swings take flight,
Gardening gloves are quite a sight.
With worms dancing in the dirt,
Even flowers wear a shirt!

When the rain starts to pour,
Umbrellas create a colorful shore.
Splashing puddles, what a show,
A ballet with shoes, on they go!

At bedtime, stories take a spin,
Adventures with dragons and ducks that grin.
With laughter echoing through the night,
Sleep, dear friend, till morning light!

A Heart's Embrace

On the sofa, juggling socks,
Tickled toes and silly talks.
With a pillow fight brewing ahead,
Who knew laughter lived in threads?

In the backyard, running free,
Chasing bubbles, what a spree!
A dog in shades, a cat on a ball,
Life's just funny—don't let it stall!

During lunch, spaghetti reigns,
Noodles dancing with no chains.
Tomato sauce flies high and wide,
We laugh until we almost cried!

As night falls, wishes take flight,
Shooting stars in the moon's light.
With giggles echoing through the dark,
Sleep brings dreams to leave a mark!

Lullabies of Solace

In the morning, pancake stacks,
With syrup rivers on our tracks.
Kids embrace the waffle game,
While the toaster steals the fame!

In the living room, toys can't hide,
Monsters zooming, full of pride.
With giggles emerging from the fray,
They plot another fun-filled day!

At dinner, forks begin to dance,
While broccoli sways in a trance.
Garlic bread clinks with delight,
Inviting laughter every bite!

When bedtime tales spin a yarn,
A dragon's sneeze clears the barn.
With bedtime kisses lingering near,
Sweet dreams, dear friends, have no fear!

Voices in Gentle Shadows

In the quiet corners, whispers roam,
They tell stories that tickle the bone.
Laughter dances on a soft breeze,
As care is wrapped in a light tease.

With coffee spills and playful wins,
Jokes are made of our daily sins.
A grand parade of socks gone stray,
Colorful chaos brightens the day.

When the sun dips low and shadows grow,
We'll giggle at places we dare not go.
It's friendship woven with silly ties,
Crafted from love, it never dies.

So here's to those who lend a hand,
In funny ways, they help us stand.
With every chuckle and playful glance,
Life's symphony becomes a dance.

Ballad of Unseen Love

In the background, where few can see,
Lies a love that's wild and totally free.
Invisible strings attach us tight,
With a wink and a grin, it feels so right.

Coffee cups clink with tales so bold,
Of the funny things that we've been told.
A treasure chest of inside jokes,
Making smiles bloom, like happy folks.

From burnt toast mornings to missed alarms,
This unseen love has all its charms.
With each quirk that we can't quite hide,
It's laughter that always turns the tide.

So let's sing this tune of unseen grace,
With silly dances, we find our place.
In awkward moments, we rise above,
Creating magic in our shared love.

Chords of Kindness

Strumming on life's old guitar,
We find our notes, no matter how far.
With each chord, a gentle hum,
Makes our hearts dance and our troubles succumb.

The beat's a mix of joy and cheer,
Accompanied by laughter we hold dear.
Silly songs in the middle of night,
Turn our worries into pure delight.

Oh, the melodies crafted with glee,
Like a playful cat climbs on our knee.
In this band of joy, every note sings,
Creating magic in the simplest things.

So let's strum these chords of light,
With humor brightening up our sight.
In this musical journey, we comprehend,
Kindness dances where laughter blends.

The Dance of Dedication

Waltzing through chaos with two left feet,
A dance of dedication can't be beat.
With every step and unexpected twirl,
We chase the challenges, give them a whirl.

In the kitchen, the floor's a stage,
While dinner bubbles, we act our age.
Spinning around with a pot in hand,
Two goofy partners in our own little band.

When the music stops, and silence reigns,
We crack a joke to bind those chains.
Every stumble shapes the dance we make,
In dedication, we're never fake.

So let's embrace this joyful chance,
With laughter leading our happy dance.
Through each misstep and spirited prance,
Life is better in this strange expanse.

Caring Notes Beneath the Stars

Under the stars so bright,
We hum a tune of care,
With coffee cups in hand,
And cookies waiting there.

Giggles echo through the night,
As band-aids get misplaced,
We try to fix a paper cut,
But end up in a race.

Whispers of wacky tales,
Fill the air with glee,
Each story gets taller,
Like a clumsy tree!

In the land of midnight snacks,
We dance and spin around,
With pets as our sidekicks,
Laughter is our sound.

Tides of Tender Care

Waves of love roll in and out,
As I splash your face with joy,
With rubber ducks a-floating,
A bath turns into a ploy.

Bubble beards and silly hats,
Make every moment grand,
We sail on silly ships,
With bath toys close at hand.

When the tide begins to rise,
And bubbles go astray,
We'll laugh until we're breathless,
At the foamy ballet!

So here we splash and sing,
In our own crazy way,
With towels on our heads,
It's the best kind of play!

Voices of the Nurturer

In kitchens bright and warm,
Voices mix like stew,
With recipes of laughter,
And love that's always new.

We whisk away the worries,
And sprinkle in some cheer,
With every quirky comment,
We bring the smiles near.

Chocolate chips in pockets,
And flour on our face,
A dance beneath the lanterns,
Turns chaos into grace.

As cookies burn in laughter,
We crack a few more jokes,
For every perfect moment,
Outweighs the cooking blokes!

Pledges of Patience

In a world of tiny toys,
And puzzles upside down,
We promise not to lose it,
When chaos comes around.

With open arms we gather,
The socks that do not pair,
We laugh at silly mix-ups,
Patience floats in the air.

When time flies like a kite,
And snacks seem to vanish fast,
We'll tickle every moment,
And let the fun outlast.

For every little challenge,
Is an adventure to embrace,
With giggles as our anchor,
Patience wears a funny face!

A Serenade for the Silent Wounds

In the kitchen, we stir up cheer,
With pots that seem to disappear.
I swear the veggies dance around,
   Making soup a circus sound.

My dance moves can't be contained,
While wiping spills, I feel unchained.
  A playlist of giggles fills the air,
  As I trip over the cat who's there.

Caring Currents

My sponge fights back -- it's quite a feat,
As dishes pile, it feels defeat.
Yet in this chaos, we find some glee,
Pretend to scrub in a jazzy spree.

Oh, look at that! A sock's found home!
It rolled away -- oh how it roamed!
With every laugh, I mend a heart,
In this crazy, wild artsy chart.

The Pulse of Understanding

Oh, the laundry's a mountain today,
I think I lost my mind in the fray.
Each shirt holds stories, wild and grand,
Like old knights, they take a stand.

When snacks go missing from the shelf,
I giggle, blame it on the elf.
For in this house, we share the weight,
Turning chores into tales of fate.

The Caress of Calm

Amidst the chaos, giggles bloom,
With every twist, we chase the gloom.
In pillow forts, we build our dreams,
As laughter floats on joyful beams.

We're sipping tea with three eyed frogs,
While dodging dust from playful dogs.
In this dance of care and craze,
We spin our love in silly ways.

Shadows of Solace

In a world of socks misplaced,
I find treasures, quite embraced.
A sandwich hidden, oh, what a bite,
Laughter echoes, pure delight.

Wobbly chairs and squeaky shoes,
Mismatched mugs of vibrant hues.
Here comes chaos, do you hear?
Just dance it off, we'll persevere!

Amidst the clutter, joy is found,
A gentle poke, a playful sound.
Chasing giggles, dodging toys,
In every mess, there's simple joys.

The laundry pile grows like a tower,
But oh, the tales of funny power.
With goofy hats and silly songs,
We find our rhythm, where laughter belongs.

A Symphony of Support

The drum of dishes clangs away,
While socks perform a ballet play.
Brooms do cha-chas, mop spins around,
In this concert, fun is found.

The cat jumps high, a star on stage,
While dinner simmers, we engage.
A pot lid claps, a spoon takes flight,
Each note is silly, pure delight.

We dance through spills, the floor's our friend,
A wacky tune that will not end.
Each hiccup forms a melody,
In this ruckus, we're wild and free.

Though life's a jam of mismatched days,
We laugh and sing in quirky ways.
With notes of chaos, love is heard,
In our symphony, hope is stirred.

Serenade of the Selfless

In pajamas worn like battle gear,
I face the morning with some cheer.
A spilled cup here, a cereal rain,
What a way to start, oh what a pain!

We juggle lunches, snacks galore,
With kiddo chaos, who could ask for more?
The sink erupts with sudsy dreams,
While laughter bubbles like flowing streams.

An afternoon of joyful strife,
A serenade of wacky life.
With hilarious tales and silly plots,
We find the fun in all the spots.

With open arms and grins so wide,
We're the wildest fun-filled ride.
In every hug and every cheer,
The selfless heart knows no fear.

The Rhythm of Resilience

In the kitchen, flour flies around,
Cookies dancing, silliness found.
A whisk break-dances, eggs on the beat,
What a party, such a treat!

Scrubbing floors to a jazzy tune,
Mops and brooms sway, oh, how they croon.
The vacuum's groan, a bass so low,
Each swipe of dust, a funky show.

Though the timer dings at crazy odds,
We juggle tasks like superhero gods.
With laughter loud and hearts so light,
We take on the day, ready to fight.

In this rhythm of loving care,
We spin and twirl, nothing to spare.
Through the chaos, we'll dance and sing,
For resilience shines in everything.

Beyond the Facade of Struggle

With a smile like butter on toast,
They juggle the tasks, an amazing host.
Band-aids and laughter, solutions galore,
Who knew caregiving could be such a chore?

They dance through the chaos, a waltz on the floor,
Trip over the toys, then they sing out 'Encore!'
Lost in the routine, but never in doubt,
'What's that underfoot?' It's a sock—freaking out!

They juggle the chaos, have fun with the fuss,
A superhero's cape is just not a must.
With humor as armor, they battle the stress,
And bless all the mishaps that turn to success.

While others may wallow in woes, dark and deep,
They find joy in each stubbing of toes, whoop!
In the circus of life, they take center stage,
Turning struggle to laughter, life's sweetest sage.

The Lantern of Love

In the kitchen, a mess like the aftermath of rain,
They whip up a feast, and ignore every stain.
The recipe reads, 'Add a dash of delight,'
And who needs a measuring cup in this fight?

With cookie dough flies and a sprinkle of cheer,
Their culinary magic elicits a tear.
And when the kids greet the food with disdain,
They laugh it off, saying, 'We'll eat it again!'

Their love lights the way, like a neon-bright buzz,
Banishing stress while they stir up the fuzz.
Who cares if the pancakes look more like blobs?
They serve all the giggles, like a buffet of sobs.

At the dinner table, chaos laughs with flair,
Spaghetti's a necklace—who knew we could wear?
With each bite, they giggle, they dance, and they cheer,
In the lantern of love, no shadows appear.

Voices of Valiance

In the morning, like clockwork, the giggles arise,
A battle of wills through wide-open eyes.
With toothbrushes raised like swords in the air,
Fighting off the dragon of 'Brush with some care!'

They stand on the frontlines of make-believe wars,
With capes made of blankets, they open the doors.
Together as heroes, they'll conquer the day,
With laughter as armor, they're never cliché.

The laundry resembles a mountain of doom,
'What's this little sock? Ah yes, it's a bloom!'
In the garden of clothes, they plant joy and fun,
Harvesting chuckles, together they run.

Each chaos-filled battle won brings forth a cheer,
The voice of valiance ringing loud and clear.
So raise high the sword, with grace we will glide,
In the realm of the brave, we forever abide.

Melting Hearts in Harmony

In a symphony of squeals, the morning begins,
With pancakes that flip like they're doing twin spins.
Syrup rivers flow, sticky fingers unite,
While laughter bursts forth like a balloon taking flight.

In the midst of the chaos, a dance in the din,
They twirl and they swirl, let the madness begin.
With giggles like jingle bells ringing so sweet,
Who knew breakfast could be such a fun treat?

With crayons on walls, artistry uncouth,
'Look, a masterpiece!' they proclaim with a tooth.
Their hearts are all melted, like chocolate in sun,
In this family of chaos, it's forever fun.

At night, as the stars twinkle up in the sky,
They tuck in each other with a friendly sigh.
The harmony sings as they drift into dreams,
For bedtime's a concert of laughter and beams.

Threads of Unseen Grace

In fluffy socks and wielding a broom,
She twirls like a dancer in a living room.
With a coffee cup full of dreams and a grin,
She juggles our mess like it's all in the spin.

Her recipes twist, they tang and they turn,
A pinch of confusion, a dash of concern.
We laugh as we soften the kitchen's big plight,
Her magic in chaos makes everything right.

Each hug is a puzzle, wrapped tenderly tight,
She solves every riddle with warmth and delight.
When socks go missing and the cat's in a flap,
She's knitting together our family's mishap.

From spilled milk explosions to chocolatey hands,
She leads us through laughter with whimsical plans.
In this dance of her life, we're all swirls and twirls,
With threads of unseen grace in our everyday curls.

A Soft Embrace of Giving

With cookies in hand and a grin ear to ear,
She conquers the kitchen with no hint of fear.
When burnt offerings come, we just chuckle and sigh,
'It's the love that counts, not the pie!' we reply.

Her advice is a riddle wrapped up with some cheer,
'Just throw in some sprinkles, make laughter the steer!'
With mischief in eyes, she plans all her pranks,
Turning chores into games, our lives full of thanks.

When life throws a curve, she catches it right,
With a wink and a laugh, turns our troubles to light.
Her hugs are like rainbows, bright, warm, and round,
In each soft embrace, there's a joy to be found.

So here's to the moments when all seems askew,
With love in her heart, she knows just what to do.
For each silly stumble and laugh that we bring,
She dances through chaos, our humorous spring.

Embracing the Weight of Worry

With a frown on her face, she plops down a stack,
Of laundry and worries — she's ready to crack.
But as she unravels her colorful plight,
She bursts out with laughter, 'What a funny sight!'

She grapples with problems like they're toys on the floor,

With giggles and grumbles, she opens the door.
'Just breathe deep and try—this seems quite absurd!'
Where laughter's the answer, she's found each word.

As she juggles our worries and bounces about,
She whispers a joke, drives our fears to shout.
'Why worry, dear child, when the world's such a jest?
Let's dance through our troubles, it's better, I guess!'

So here's to the weight she embraces each day,
Turning burdens to light in her whimsical way.
With a wink and a smile, she says, 'Not a thing,
Can dampen our spirits—let's twirl and let's swing!'

The Compass of Empathy

In the land of the grumpy, she wears a bright hat,
Offering hugs to even the thorns and the brats.
With a tickle and tease, she brightens the frown,
Like a sunny disco ball spinning round and round.

Her jokes lift the mood like a warm summer breeze,
She dances through sorrows with charm and with ease.
'What's life without laughter?' she quips with a grin,
As we roll in the aisles, our true joy begins.

With her compass of empathy, guiding us all,
She navigates hearts—never stoops, never stalls.
Her laughter's a lighthouse, so bright and so clear,
In the stormiest seas, it's her song that we hear.

So here's to the moments when kindness prevails,
With her at the helm, we'll ride all the gales.
With warmth in her heart and silliness too,
She steers us through life, her laughter our crew.

The Dance of Dedication

In slippers worn, they glide and sway,
With mismatched socks, they laugh and play.
A cereal spill, a rubber duck,
They twirl in chaos, oh what luck!

The laundry spins like a dizzy track,
As they chase the cat who won't look back.
With giggles loud, and silly moves,
They dance in tune that nothing proves!

An apron on, a hat askew,
Making dinner for the zoo.
The broccoli smiles, the carrots cheer,
In this grand feast, all's welcome here!

With each silly step, they find the beat,
While tripping on shoes that are too neat.
Laughter echoes, the room alights,
In the dance of love, our hearts take flight.

Paths of Compassionate Light

Through muddy paths, with boots of cheer,
They navigate life, year after year.
In puddles splash, they laugh aloud,
Turning woes to joy, oh so proud!

With heartfelt tales and quirky glee,
They offer hugs, how sweet it be!
A broken toy, a chocolate bar,
Transforming frowns, their power's bizarre!

They skip through thorns, dodging care,
With jokes to share, they light the air.
Compassion glows like fireflies bright,
In every step, they spread pure light!

As shadows dance and worries fade,
They wear their hearts like a grand parade.
With laughter ringing, life takes flight,
On paths where joy and mirth ignite.

Dreaming in Diligence

With sleepy eyes, they brew a cup,
A splash of coffee, and then a sup.
"Rise and shine!" they cheer with zest,
While buttoning up a mismatched vest.

To-do lists dance like lively bees,
With quirky doodles that aim to please.
The vacuum hums like a groovy band,
While socks go missing, not quite planned!

Diligence mixed with daydreams bright,
Turns chores to fun, what sheer delight!
As laundry spins, so too do they,
In a whirlwind of laughter, life at play!

When midnight strikes, they still persist,
A heroic bindle, nothing missed.
In dreams they wander, off they go,
With silly tales of socks in tow!

Lyrical Lives United

In a circle, they sing with flair,
Voices blending in the air.
The dog joins in with a howl so proud,
As they giggle with the playful crowd.

With every note, they twirl around,
Turning frowns to smiles profound.
A rhythm born from sweet embrace,
In silly spins, they find their place!

Together they weave a vibrant scene,
With pizza slices and math that's mean.
From bedtime tales to morning glory,
Each moment shared tells a funny story!

In laughter's arms, they firmly stand,
An ode to life, oh isn't it grand?
With joyful hearts, they take the stage,
In lyrical lives, they turn the page!

The Light in Their Eyes

In the morning they bound and leap,
With giggles that tickle, their joy runs deep.
Like squirrels with snacks, they veer and dart,
A dance of chaos, a comedy art.

With soup on the ceiling, we laugh and twirl,
Sprinkled with mayhem, our plans now unfurl.
Their laughter's a melody, silly and bright,
Even when spaghetti takes flight in the night.

In mismatched socks, they lead the parade,
Each step a new joke, under sunshine laid.
We march to our rhythm, as silly tunes play,
In this circus of life, we're clowns every day.

So here's to the light that they bring all around,
In a world full of giggles, true joy can be found.
With hugs that can power a hundred small wheels,
My heart sings with laughter; oh, how good it feels!

Songs of Resilience

Oh, the tales these little ones weave,
With capes made of sheets, they're kings and thieves.
In battles with dragons and monsters in sight,
They charge with their courage; it's quite a delight.

With every minor scrape, they craft their own plan,
Mixing band-aids with giggles, like only they can.
A superhero's armor, so bright and so bold,
In a world filled with wonder, their laughter we hold.

Through puddles they leap, each splash a loud cheer,
As if winning a trophy for wiping our tears.
In the busyness of life, they teach us to play,
Each moment a treasure that brightens our day.

With songs of resilience, they show us the way,
To dance through the storms, come what may.
Their joy is a lesson; their light a great prize,
In the heart of a child, a strength that defies!

Cadence of Comfort

In the chaos of crayons, and dolls in a row,
Amidst laughter, they find comfort in the flow.
Like music they hum, each note a delight,
Creating a world where worries take flight.

With tickles and tea parties, they rule the abode,
Their giggles a symphony, a soothing code.
From messes and mishaps, they craft their own rhyme,
In the cadence of comfort, they conquer time.

Potato sack races in soft, sunny light,
With champions crowned in pajamas each night.
Oops! There goes supper, the dog joins the spree,
Part chef, part comedian, oh how they're free!

In this grand adventure of mound and of mess,
They cherish each moment, they truly impress.
With the beat of their hearts and the joy in their rooms,
They sing us a lullaby that sweetly resumes!

Hymns of Hope

In a kingdom of toys, where rules don't apply,
They build dreams with laughter, oh my, oh my!
With pies made of clouds and worlds made of fun,
Every day's magic—until they are done!

With legos and laughter, they fashion their throne,
Where whispers of hope are triumphantly grown.
Through fortresses fashioned of sheets and of chairs,
They teach us that joy can flow from their snares.

When clouds roll in dark and the rain starts to pour,
They dance in the puddles while hearts cry for more.
With smiles like sunshine, they brighten the gloom,
In their hymns of hope, flowers begin to bloom.

So here's to the spirits who refuse to fade,
In a world where they're gleeful, no price can be paid.
For the laughter they carry, like bubbles in flight,
In their joyous embrace, every wrong feels so right!

Garden of Gentle Souls

In a garden where laughter grows,
We water joy with silly prose.
Pulling weeds of worry away,
Planting smiles to light the day.

Whispers of giggles fill the air,
As sunshine winks without a care.
Butterflies dance on a breeze,
While squirrels plot their nutty schemes.

Underneath the shade of a tree,
What a sight, come laugh with me!
With playful banter, hearts align,
A patchwork quilt of love divine.

In our silly little nook,
Each petal shares a happy look.
From daisies bright to roses bold,
A garden where warmth will unfold.

Tapestry of Tender Moments

Stitching smiles with threads of gold,
In this crazy tale we're told.
Each moment a pattern, each laugh a thread,
A patchwork tale of joy widespread.

Poking fun at life's small quirks,
In the fabric where laughter lurks.
With twine of kindness, we weave along,
Creating a tapestry so strong.

Patterns twist and turn with glee,
While adding oddities, just wait and see!
A crooked seam? Oh, who really cares?
It's the laughter that lifts us, like fresh air.

Each snip and stitch tells a tale,
In this wondrous giggle gale.
Together we laugh, together we mend,
In threads of joy, our hearts transcend.

Balancing Act of Love

On a tightrope made of silly grins,
Doing backflips, where the fun begins.
Juggling hearts like they're rubber balls,
In this circus where laughter calls.

Monkeys swing with giddy cheer,
Joking that balance is quite unclear.
With each wobble comes a laugh,
Turning blunders into autograph.

Clown shoes on, we dance around,
As joy and giggles fiercely abound.
In this act, we sway and spin,
Where love and laughter always win.

So come and join this wacky show,
With every slip, 'gainst gravity we throw.
In this balancing act, we do declare,
Happiness thrives in the lightness of air.

The Wish of a Caregiver

Wishing for giggles in a world of sighs,
With silly hats and playful ties.
A sprinkle of humor, a dash of cheer,
Transforming the ordinary, we hold dear.

Every wish sprinkled with love's embrace,
Turns heavy burdens into a dance space.
To tickle frowns and giggle at fears,
Creating magic that lasts through years.

A little bit of fun in each tender deed,
Like planting a seed, it's all that we need.
Dreams delivered with laughter's delight,
Chasing away shadows, igniting the night.

So here's my wish wrapped up with a bow,
That joy finds us wherever we go.
With each chuckle, we light up the way,
In a world where smiles happily stay.

Love's Quiet Anthem

In the kitchen, drama stirs,
A spatula flings past my ears.
Dinner's burnt but hearts still smile,
Laughter echoes, let's stay awhile.

Socks are mismatched, that's no crime,
Dancing through chaos, what a time!
With each slip and every trip,
We find joy in each little quip.

Tea spills down the counter wide,
Yet with a chuckle, we take it in stride.
A pillow fort under the stairs,
A fortress built with giggles and cares.

Rhythms of Understanding

I tune my heart to the toddler's beat,
As crayons scribble on the seat.
Their little giggles in perfect rhyme,
We dance and stumble, lost in time.

Fingers sticky with jam and glee,
Who knew snack time could set us free?
In between bites, we share our dreams,
Chasing bubbles, bursting seams.

The world's a stage of slapstick grace,
As I chase after a runaway pace.
Yet with each blooper, a lesson learned,
In this rhythm, our hearts have turned.

Notes from a Caring Heart

With a yo-yo in hand, I give it a try,
It may drop down, but we'll laugh, oh my!
In the mess, there's beauty, we find,
In the chords of chaos, joy intertwined.

Cookies crumble, flour takes flight,
Our kitchen's a battleground tonight!
But every giggle makes it worthwhile,
As we clean up the mess with a smile.

In the symphony of hugs and tears,
We craft our song through the silly years.
With every note, we learn to play,
In this concert of love, come what may.

A Tapestry of Warmth

On a cold night, our blanket's a fort,
With a flashlight we create our own court.
Stories told with exaggerated flair,
Monsters lurk, but we're not scared!

Each sneeze is met with a grand parade,
As I hunt for tissues, they won't evade.
A symphony of snorts fills the air,
An orchestra of germs, we boldly share!

Through the tickles and tussles, love's our glue,
In the rhythm of life, we know it's true.
With laughter entwined, our hearts remain warm,
A tapestry woven, a perfect charm.

Reflections of a Guardian

In the chaos of toys, I trip and I fall,
Dodging Legos like arrows, I'm having a ball.
With snacks in my pocket, I play Simon Says,
Pretending to be cool, while hiding the mess.

I sing silly songs that don't rhyme at all,
As laughter erupts from my short, squishy hall.
Juggling their whims, like a clown in disguise,
I wear my best smile while dodging their cries.

Spilling the juice, oh! What a delightful tale,
Chasing runaway kittens, I'm destined to fail.
With bubble baths shared and pajamas on tight,
We giggle and dance in the soft, evening light.

So here's to the giggles and moments we keep,
In the heart of this chaos, my soul takes a leap.
These days may be messy, yet filled with delight,
For memories sparkle like stars in the night.

The Light of Quiet Devotion

Quietly I shuffle, avoiding the squeaks,
Tiptoeing on floors that have lost their mystique.
With a snack in my pocket, I make my grand round,
In a world full of noise, I am under profound.

They leave little treasures, those toys on the floor,
Each step a new dance; oh, what's in store?
I tip over blocks, I trip over shoes,
While crafting fine stories with ridiculous hues.

With ice cream for dinner, their giggles take flight,
I hide my own joy behind playful fright.
They spin and they whirl, a tornado of fun,
In this whirlwind of love, we're all number one.

When bedtime arrives, it's a mystical quest,
To read one more story before they get rest.
With a wink and a nod, I wonder out loud,
Who's really the caregiver? I feel so proud.

Verses of Vigilance

Peering around corners, I tiptoe with flair,
Where did they run off? I must seek with care.
With snacks in my arsenal, I track down the horde,
In this wild little jungle, I pull out my sword.

They've hidden away treasures, much like silent ninjas,
I'm searching for quiet, but they're spreading their fingers.
With laughter like thunder and mischief galore,
My heart swells with joy; love's an endless score.

I juggle their antics, like pies in the air,
Each giggle a gift that I'm eager to share.
As the clock ticks away, I feel time slip by,
In this circus of laughter, I'm learning to fly.

In the heart of this ruckus, love shines like the sun,
For every lost shoe, it's just more silly fun.
So here's to the chaos, the giggles, the screams,
In this wild, vibrant dance, we're living our dreams.

A Song for the Weary

Oh, what a day, full of giggles and yells,
With crumbs on the couch, can you hear the bells?
From breakfast to bedtime, the chaos is real,
But in every lost sock is a treasure I feel.

With stories of giants and heroes so grand,
I'm trapped in the tales they invent on demand.
I laugh and I sigh at their whims and their grins,
For the joy that they bring makes my heart spin.

As dinner turns mayhem, spaghetti takes flight,
With sauce on my forehead, it's quite the sight!
Their giggles erupt like balloons in the air,
In the midst of the chaos, love dances with flair.

So here's to the weary, the brave and the bold,
In a life full of laughter, our stories unfold.
With a wink and a nudge, may we always sing,
Of love wrapped in play, it's a magical thing.

Kindness in Every Breath

In a world of chaos, a nurse misplaces,
Stethoscopes in pockets, with curious graces.
Patients giggle at the sight so rare,
As he checks for heartbeats in the wrong hair.

With band-aids sticking to his shoe,
He laughs out loud; oh, what a view!
Mixes up jello with the IV drip,
Serves dessert, then takes a sip!

His smile brightens the dreariest days,
Filling the room with his quirky ways.
A dance in the hallway, a spin and a twirl,
Transforming a frown with a playful whirl.

So here's to the laughter, the joy they bring,
With hugs and silly songs that make hearts sing.
In every breath, kindness is found,
In the laughter shared, life spins around.

Nature's Guardian

A doctor runs late, birds sing and cheer,
His stethoscope tangled in grapevine near.
While checking a pulse, he finds a bug,
Instead of a heart, he gives it a hug!

In scrubs turning green like the leaves in spring,
He quips with a patient, "Isn't life zing?"
In the waiting room, the flowers all bloom,
With jokes 'bout pollen that lighten the gloom.

A gardener at heart, he tends to the ill,
Watering laughter; oh, what a thrill!
With each silly story he loves to impart,
He nurtures their spirits, a seed for the heart.

Nature's own helper, he prances about,
Finding humor in life's smallest route.
In charts filled with laughter, he draws a great smile,
For healing with giggles can go quite a mile!

In the Arms of Comfort

A nurse with a cape, thinks she's a hero,
Turns out she's great at catching a zero.
With tissues in pockets and soup on her shoes,
She melts all the worries, brightens the blues.

In a padded chair with a patient or two,
She tells of the day when a cat learned to chew.
With pillows that squeak and a blanket that snorts,
She crafts a warm haven with cozy reports.

A hug full of giggles, she hands out with flair,
With each hearty laugh, she lightens the air.
Mismatched her socks, what a colorful sight,
Making each moment a tickle of light.

Under bright posters, she dances with glee,
"Let's hum a tune; who's the best at a spree?"
In arms of comfort, the spirits ascend,
With moments of silliness, laughter won't end.

The Solace of Presence

A doctor appears with a quirky surprise,
A rubber chicken under the skies.
While checking your vitals, don't mind the beak,
With laughter he shows that it's okay to peek.

In the clinic, one patient pulls a bad prank,
Pretending to faint, but that's not his rank.
With a wink and a giggle, he plays along fast,
Together they laugh, it's a moment that lasts.

In slippers instead of shoes, he strolls around,
Feet all grown tired, but joy is profound.
With each silly question, the heaviness fades,
Making room for laughter, no need for charades.

In the solace of presence, they kindle a spark,
With pistachio ice cream, they brighten the dark.
For in every chuckle lies healing's true ace,
With humor and joy, they weave a warm space.

A Chorus of Kindness

In a house full of giggles, they play all day,
With socks on their hands, they dance and sway.
Mixing up soup with a splash of fun,
They tell silly stories until the day's done.

Juggling the chores like a circus act,
With a grin on their face and a joyful pact.
Whisking up laughter, they never lose sight,
Of how silly life is when you dance with delight.

The cat wears a hat, it's a fully-fledged show,
As they twirl and they twinkle, with sweet-hearted glow.
Knitting warm hugs that tickle and tease,
Life's a grand stage, come laugh with such ease!

Baking some cookies, a mess on the floor,
With sprinkles that fly like fireworks galore.
They sing silly songs that inspire a grin,
Join this mad chorus, let the joy spin!

Gentle Hands in Quietude

In the quiet of morning, they start with a plan,
To turn every task into a whimsical span.
With dusters a-dancing and brooms that hum,
They rock out their chores, oh what silly fun!

Feeding the birds with a sprinkle of cheer,
Every crumb tossed is met with a cheer.
While folding up laundry, they play peek-a-boo,
A laundry sock war, just for laughs, who knew?

The plants wear little hats, so chic and so bright,
Watering them with joy, a peculiar sight.
A gentle parade down the hallway they stroll,
With giggles and grins, their hearts are the goal.

As the sun sets low, they dim the great light,
A shadow puppet show is their favorite delight.
With gentle hands crafting silly old tales,
They find pure joy in their quirky details!

Melodies of Compassion

A piano that squeaks with each playful touch,
They tickle those keys, giggling oh so much.
Singing off-key yet with heart wide and true,
Each note like a hug wrapped in joy that they brew.

In the garden they dance, a flower parade,
With watering cans making tunes in the shade.
A sunflower bows low, it can hardly keep still,
As laughter blooms brightly, what a joyous thrill!

They serenade critters with songs of delight,
From raccoons to rabbits, they join in the night.
With care and with charm, they twirl and they sway,
Creating sweet melodies to brighten the day.

Twirling around as the fireflies glow,
In harmony, sharing the warmth of the flow.
With kindness in rhythm and love in the air,
Every note sings out, life's a magical flair!

Echoes of Tenderness

Whisking up trouble in their favorite boots,
They march to the rhythm of giggly pursuits.
Mixing up giggles and sprinkles galore,
Echoes of laughter, they'll always implore.

Turning old chairs into musical thrones,
Holding grand concerts with pots, pans, and tones.
With squeaky voices that break all the rules,
In this kingdom of laughter, they reign as the fools!

A parade of socks dancing here and there,
With ribbons and bows, a funny affair.
Each silly step makes their hearts feel so light,
Celebrating the joy in this whimsical night.

As the stars sprinkle joy on their playful spree,
Together they laugh, oh what sights they see!
In this echo of kindness, they find their way,
In a world full of giggles that brighten their day!

The Heart's Garden

In a garden where laughter grows,
They dance with weeds and giggle in rows.
Petunias wear tutus, tulips in hats,
Sunflowers sway, sharing jokes with the cats.

Bunnies in boots hop with delight,
Chasing each other, what a sight!
With gloves on their ears, they prance and sing,
The gardener chuckles—what joy they bring!

Bees buzz in rhythm, a comical song,
While vegetables cheer, 'Come join our throng!'
Carrots play tag with the chubby peas,
In this heart's garden, it's all fun and ease.

With petals of laughter and roots of cheer,
They tend to the blooms without any fear.
In the heart's own patch, joy always thrives,
Encouraging giggles, that's how it survives!

Graced with Giving

A pot of soup, a dash of zest,
With a side of laughter, that's truly the best.
Carrots that wiggle, onions that dance,
Each ladle of magic gets all in a trance.

Cookies that giggle, they'll melt in your hand,
Sprinkled with mischief, just as planned.
Great-aunt's old recipe, a hoot in the mix,
A pinch of joy, with outrageous fix!

Baked goods gossip while cooling on shelves,
'Who will taste us? Well, we can't tell!'
Sugar levels soaring, laughter in the air,
This giving feels magical, beyond compare.

With every crumb shared, joy multiplies,
In this kitchen of heart, oh, what a surprise!
Cooked with a giggle, served with delight,
Graced with giving, every bite takes flight!

A Songbird's Softness

In the branches, birdies crack jokes,
Fluffy little comedians, feathered folks.
With chirps and tweets, they sing a tune,
A symphony of giggles beneath the moon.

Sparrows in ties, wrens in bow ties,
Clowns of the skies with sparkly eyes.
They flap and flutter, a gaggle of glee,
Telling wild tales while sipping their tea.

The crow caws comedy, the robin applauds,
While the finch strums a tune, taking on the odds.
A fiesta of feathers, so silly, so bright,
In the songbird's chorus, everything feels right.

As twilight dances, their laughter will soar,
A melody of joy, who could ask for more?
In this sweet concert, the world feels so fine,
With a songbird's laughter, life's a divine!

Stitched in Solitude

In my cozy room, I craft a sweet quilt,
Each square a memory, every thread built.
With mismatched patterns and giggles galore,
Sewing up laughter, I couldn't ask for more.

Buttons as eyes, they wink as I sew,
Fabric dancing with stories to show.
Thimble on my finger, I sing and I grin,
Creating a tapestry where joy can begin.

Socks that once wandered are stitched with deep care,
Now cuddle together, a whimsical pair.
Patches of sunshine on a rainy old day,
Stitched in solitude, bright colors display.

With each loving stitch, I laugh to myself,
What a delightful way to brighten a shelf!
In this quiet corner, my heart finds a home,
Knitting together a world of my own.

The Weaving of Comfort

In scrubs and mismatched socks, she flies,
With spills of juice and doughnuts, oh my!
Her phone buzzes tales of chaos and cheer,
As laughter springs forth, both far and near.

With a wink and a grin, she dances with haste,
Balloons and band-aids, no need for a waste.
She juggles the meds, a circus delight,
While humming a tune that feels just right.

Her laughter's a balm, her humor a thread,
Weaving comfort with each little spread.
In the room full of giggles, she shines like a star,
Delivering joy, no matter how far.

So here's to the joy in the care that she gives,
With heart as her compass, that's how she lives!
Through each silly mishap, she finds the sweet peace,
In the weaving of comfort, her grace never cease.

Cadence of Connection

With eyebrows raised, she spins a tall tale,
Of mysterious germs and heroic scale.
Every sneeze and sniffle gets met with delight,
In her world of giggles, all will be right.

Check the pulse with a tickle and wink,
Stethoscope whispers, 'Don't you dare think!'
She dances between the beds, all aglow,
Turning woes to laughs, putting on a show.

With each little laugh and a knowing glance,
Patients forget their worries, they prance.
A spoonful of sugar, she boldly prescribes,
Mixing care with humor, in all her vibes.

Her symphony plays, with each gentle touch,
A cadence that sings, and it means so much.
In her world, kindness is the melody sweet,
Creating connections, where laughter and care meet.

The Art of Compassion

With a paintbrush and laughter, she colors the day,
Creating a canvas in a whimsical way.
Her heart spills over with hues of good cheer,
As each patient's smile makes the burdens unclear.

She crafts little jokes from the quirks they all wear,
Like mismatched socks or a wild, crazy hair.
A band-aid becomes an award of great worth,
When she crowns each sad heart, unearthing their mirth.

In the gallery of kindness, she leads the parade,
With warmth in her laughter, all sorrows she'll trade.
Painting joy and connection, her brush strokes a song,
In the art of compassion, where we all belong.

So let's raise a toast, to her art so divine,
With laughter and love, every moment's a sign.
Through splashes of joy, she creates from the heart,
And with every creation, she plays her sweet part.

Echoing Heartbeats

In the chaotic rhythm of a bustling ward,
She taps her feet, to the beat, no sword.
With a tickle of humor through every sigh,
Her joy is contagious, watch the spirits fly.

A heartbeat echoed in the laughter shared,
Her patients find solace, feeling truly cared.
With jokes as her tools, she knits bonds so tight,
Sewing up worries with laughter, pure light.

From bingo games to the wild snacks she'll bring,
Each moment is golden, an unscripted fling.
She mingles through stories, all stemming from grace,
In the echoes of heartbeats, she finds her place.

So here's to the giggles, and joy she bestows,
In the rhythm of care, her deep kindness flows.
With every pulse bounding, she dances along,
In the echoing heartbeats, we all share a song.

Radiance in the Night

In the dark, I trip on a shoe,
Bouncing back with a laugh or two.
Juggling snacks with a baby in tow,
Who knew care could spark such a show?

Wiping noses while wearing a grin,
A circus act that I can't begin.
Dodging toys, oh what a sight,
The chaos blooms, yet feels so right.

Chatting softly to tired eyes,
With silly faces to block the cries.
Kites made of blankets, we play hide and seek,
Laughter erupts, though movement is meek.

When bedtime calls, chaos must cease,
But I'll sneak in a dance for a moment of peace.
Their giggles echo, a sweet serenade,
In the night's soft hugs, my worries fade.

Flourish of the Devoted

Chasing after socks that don't match,
Tickling toes that I can't catch.
With band-aids ready, I save the day,
As chocolate spills in a 'professional' way.

A potion mix of juice and cheer,
The kids all cheer, for it's that time of year!
Silly hats and capes on parade,
A moment of glee, together we've made.

Mismatched meals on the kitchen floor,
"Who wants veggies?" I hear a roar.
Crafting futures with glitter and glue,
In our chaotic realm, it's a vibrant view.

So here I stand, my apron askew,
Like a fearless leader in a colorful zoo.
With laughter as our favorite song,
In this wild, funny life, we all belong.

A Journey of Care

Up the stairs, a race begins,
Who can reach the top? Oh, what sins!
With a superhero cape and charm like no other,
We dive into chaos, sister and brother.

'Time for fierce hugs!' I loudly declare,
And suddenly we're flying through the air.
Screams burst forth like fireworks bright,
As bedtime stories are lost in the night.

Squishy faces and silly sounds,
A rollercoaster ride of love abounds.
Pajamas tangled in a knotty embrace,
Each moment of joy, a warm, cozy place.

And when the stars twinkle in the sky,
With ruffled heads, we let out a sigh.
The journey of care, with giggles and play,
In this wacky world, we find our way.

Verses of Vigilance

Eyes wide open, a watchful gaze,
As a cheese monster lurks in the maze.
With spatula swords, we fight with glee,
In this kitchen battle, there's laughter for free.

Tiny hands reaching for a cookie jar,
A stealthy mission, my little star.
Camouflage in pajamas, a covert affair,
Who's the sneakiest? We're quite the pair!

With crayons flying and paper galore,
The masterpiece leaks right out the door.
I step in paint, a colorful truce,
Embracing the mess, and setting it loose.

At day's end, a tired cheer,
I gather them close, their giggles sincere.
In this waltz of care, I take my stand,
Laughing through love, hand in hand.

www.ingramcontent.com/pod-product-compliance
Lightning Source LLC
Chambersburg PA
CBHW070310120526
44590CB00017B/2611